This journal belongs to

May the pages of this journal be filled with heartfelt conversations with our Heavenly Father!

I dedicate this Prayer Journal to the memory of my beloved Mother, Ima Lois Chimney Lampkin, a woman of much prayer. Her commitment to a lifestyle of prayer was rooted in her understanding of the need to pray.

As far back as I can remember, my Mother exemplified exceptional discipline, demonstrating the power of consistent and fervent prayer. Her steadfast devotion taught my sister and me the importance of pursuing God's presence in every circumstance.

Ima Lois Chimney Lampkin, a woman of great faith and power, left an indelible mark on my soul. Her legacy of prayer continues to inspire and guide me by reminding me of the necessity of communion with our Heavenly Father.

Dearest Mother, thank you for imparting your love of prayer to me. Your legacy lives on, and I am forever grateful for the immeasurable gift of you.

Welcome

Welcome to your 90-Day Prayer Journal! This journal serves a twofold purpose: to encourage and challenge you to embark on a season of consistent prayer, and to assist you in fostering a deeper connection with God. By committing to this process, you are prioritizing prayer. This journal is a tool in your spiritual journey, guiding you closer to the Lord and equipping you to experience the transformative power of prayer. May these 90 days be a time of growth, revelation, and encounters with God.

Prayer is not a mere religious duty, but a pathway to connect with our Heavenly Father and align ourselves with His divine will. At its core, prayer is communicating with God. As you embark on this 90-day journey, may this journal become your faithful companion and trusted guide. May it ignite a renewed passion and commitment for prayer, enabling you to draw closer to God and experience His presence in profound, life-changing ways.

In our fast-paced and demanding world, neglecting consistent prayer is easy. However, by embarking on this transformative 90-day journey, you are prioritizing your relationship with God. This decision is an act of faith, demonstrating your desire for a more intimate connection with your Heavenly Father. By committing to this journey, you are cultivating a lifestyle of prayer. May this journey fortify your resolve to make prayer a consistent part of your daily life.

Within the pages of this journal, you will discover an invitation to open your heart and pour out your deepest thoughts and desires to God. Each day, you will find carefully crafted prompts and ample space to express your gratitude, present your requests, and listen attentively to God's voice. Through the consistent practice of these exercises, you will embark on a journey that will deepen your intimacy with God and unveil the transformative power of prayer in your life. As you engage, you will experience the impact of consistent prayer. Get ready to encounter the Father as you commune with Him through the pages of this journal.

Prayers and Petitions

To begin, take a moment to write down your prayer requests. Remember, no request is too big or too small for God. The Bible assures us in 1 John 5:15, "And if we know that he hears us—whatever we ask—we know that we have what we asked of him." Journaling your requests brings clarity and focus, and allows you to document your petitions before the Lord. One of the definitions of a petition is a formal written request; thus, your written prayers become a tangible expression of your faith and trust in God. So, take this opportunity to pour out your heart and commit your desires to Him.

Align Your Prayers

Next, search the Bible for at least three scriptures that align with your prayer requests. Look for verses that speak directly to your desires and allow these scriptures to guide your prayers. By praying the Word of God, you anchor your petitions in His promises and align your prayers with His will. For instance, if you seek healing, James 5:15 declares, "And the prayer of faith will save the one who is sick, and the Lord will raise him up." As you incorporate scriptures into your prayers, you declare God's promises and strengthen your faith in His ability to answer. Praying the Word of God ensures that your prayers are grounded in truth and are in harmony with His divine purpose.

Listen and Write

Thirdly, it is essential to document and pay attention to God's response. Prayer is not a one-way conversation; it involves speaking to God and listening to His voice. It is a divine dialogue, not a monologue. As you pray, meditate on the Word of God and open your heart to hear what the Holy Spirit is saying. Just as you pour out your heart to God, give equal time and attention to listen for His response. Journaling His words will help you remember and reflect upon them later. Sometimes, God may speak in ways that require you to adjust how you pray or shift your perspective. Hearing His voice brings greater intimacy and trust in your relationship with Him. Be attentive and allow His words to strengthen your faith and guide your prayers.

Remember, this journey may require repeating the first three steps multiple times. Persistence in prayer is paramount, especially when facing weariness or discouragement. The enemy may try to hinder your progress and cause you to lose heart, but do not give in. The Bible encourages us, "Let us not become weary in doing good, for at the proper time we will reap a harvest if we do not give up" (Galatians 6:9, NIV). Stay steadfast and continue pressing on, for your breakthrough is closer than you think.

Answered Prayer

This next step is exciting— God has answered your prayer! Pause and give thanks to God, who always fulfills His promises. It is vital to acknowledge and track each answered prayer. As the psalmist beautifully expressed, "Oh, that mankind would praise the LORD for his goodness and for his wonderful works to the children of men!" (Psalm 107:21). Let this verse resonate in your heart as a reminder to offer praise to God for His goodness and the miraculous ways He works in our lives.

Stones of Remembrance

Finally, create stones of remembrance. Stones of remembrance are physical objects or markers that remind us of significant life events or experiences. They can take many forms, such as actual stones, written journals, photographs, or other objects of personal significance. These stones represent moments when we have experienced God's grace, provision, healing, or deliverance.

This journal is a collection of prayers and your stones of remembrance. Each step from "asked prayer" to "answered prayer" is significant. These stones are powerful reminders of God's faithfulness and provision in your life. As you document your prayers and experiences, you are creating a legacy that can inspire and guide others. Remember that God operates on His timeline, which may not always align with our expectations. He answers based on His sovereign will. However, it is important to document the entire process—the prayers, the waiting, the lessons learned, and the growth experienced. Every stone in this journal has a story and a lesson to impart. May these stones of remembrance serve as a testament to God's faithfulness, not only in your life, but also as a source of encouragement and inspiration for others on their journey of faith.

Committing to these 90 days of prayer is a renewed covenant between you and God. When you draw near to Him, He faithfully draws near to you. These stones will help you remember God's faithfulness, strengthen your faith, and encourage others in their spiritual walk. With each stone collected, you are building a spiritual legacy that testifies to God's goodness and grace in your life.

So, remember that this journal is more than a book of prayers; it is an invitation to connect with God on a deeper level. It is an opportunity to carve out sacred moments in your day to commune with Him, to seek His face, and to experience His presence. Let this journal be a catalyst for spiritual growth and a reminder of the incredible privilege we have in prayer.

PRAYER JOURNAL
Day 1

DATE _____

S M T W T F S

PRAYER REQUESTS

- _____
- _____
- _____

- _____
- _____
- _____

SCRIPTURE REFERENCES

_____
_____
_____
_____
_____
_____

GOD'S RESPONSE

_____
_____
_____
_____
_____
_____
_____

> Therefore I say unto you, What things soever ye desire, when ye pray, believe that ye receive them, and ye shall have them.
> **MARK 11:24 KJV**

Stones of Remembrance

DATE _____

S M T W T F S

ANSWERED PRAYER

REMEMBRANCE

___

ANSWERED PRAYER

REMEMBRANCE

> And if we know that he hear us, whatsoever we ask, we know that we have the petitions that we desired of him.
> 1 JOHN 5:15

PRAYER JOURNAL
Day 2

DATE _____

S M T W T F S

PRAYER REQUESTS

- _____
- _____
- _____
- _____
- _____
- _____

SCRIPTURE REFERENCES

_____
_____
_____
_____
_____
_____

GOD'S RESPONSE

_____
_____
_____
_____
_____

> "Be careful for nothing; but in every thing by prayer and supplication with thanksgiving let your requests be made known unto God. And the peace of God, which passeth all understanding, shall keep your hearts and minds through Christ Jesus.
>
> PHILIPPIANS 4:6-7

DATE _____

S M T W T F S

ANSWERED PRAYER

REMEMBRANCE

_____
_____
_____

ANSWERED PRAYER

REMEMBRANCE

_____
_____
_____

> " But verily God hath heard me; he hath attended to the voice of my prayer.
> Blessed be God, which hath not turned away my prayer,
> nor his mercy from me.
>
> PSALM 66:19-20 "

PRAYER JOURNAL
Day 3

DATE _____

S M T W T F S

PRAYER REQUESTS

- _____
- _____
- _____
- _____
- _____
- _____

SCRIPTURE REFERENCES

_____
_____
_____
_____
_____
_____

GOD'S RESPONSE

_____
_____
_____
_____
_____
_____

Call unto me, and I will answer thee, and show thee great and mighty things, which thou knowest not.

JEREMIAH 33:3

DATE

S M T W T F S

ANSWERED PRAYER

REMEMBRANCE

ANSWERED PRAYER

REMEMBRANCE

> "For the eyes of the Lord are over the righteous, and his ears are open unto their prayers: but the face of the Lord is against them that do evil.
> 1 PETER 3:12

PRAYER JOURNAL
Day 4

DATE _____

S M T W T F S

PRAYER REQUESTS

- _____
- _____
- _____
- _____
- _____
- _____

SCRIPTURE REFERENCES

_____
_____
_____
_____
_____
_____

GOD'S RESPONSE

_____
_____
_____
_____
_____
_____

> And all things, whatsoever ye shall ask in prayer, believing, ye shall receive.
> MATTHEW 21:22

Stones of Remembrance

DATE _____

S M T W T F S

ANSWERED PRAYER

REMEMBRANCE

ANSWERED PRAYER

REMEMBRANCE

 The righteous cry, and the LORD heareth, and delivereth them out of all their troubles.
PSALM 34:17

PRAYER JOURNAL
Day 5

DATE _____

S M T W T F S

PRAYER REQUESTS

- _____
- _____
- _____
- _____
- _____
- _____

SCRIPTURE REFERENCES

_____
_____
_____
_____
_____
_____

GOD'S RESPONSE

_____
_____
_____
_____
_____
_____

 And whatsoever we ask, we receive of him, because we keep his commandments, and do those things that are pleasing in his sight.
1 JOHN 3:22

DATE _____

S M T W T F S

ANSWERED PRAYER

REMEMBRANCE

ANSWERED PRAYER

REMEMBRANCE

 O thou that hearest prayer, unto thee shall all flesh come.
PSALM 65:2

PRAYER JOURNAL
Day 6

DATE _____

S M T W T F S

PRAYER REQUESTS

- _____
- _____
- _____

- _____
- _____
- _____

SCRIPTURE REFERENCES

_____
_____
_____
_____
_____
_____

GOD'S RESPONSE

_____
_____
_____
_____
_____
_____

> *If ye shall ask any thing in my name, I will do it.*
> JOHN 14:14

Stones of Remembrance

DATE _____

S M T W T F S

ANSWERED PRAYER

REMEMBRANCE

_____
_____
_____
_____

ANSWERED PRAYER

REMEMBRANCE

_____
_____
_____
_____

> Then shall ye call upon me, and ye shall go and pray unto me, and I will hearken unto you.
> **JEREMIAH 29:12**

PRAYER JOURNAL
Day 7

DATE _____

S M T W T F S

PRAYER REQUESTS

- _____
- _____
- _____
- _____
- _____
- _____

SCRIPTURE REFERENCES

_____
_____
_____
_____
_____
_____

GOD'S RESPONSE

_____
_____
_____
_____
_____
_____

> Ask, and it shall be given you; seek, and ye shall find; knock, and it shall be opened unto you
> MATTHEW 7:7

DATE

S M T W T F S

ANSWERED PRAYER

REMEMBRANCE

ANSWERED PRAYER

REMEMBRANCE

> "For every one that asketh receiveth; and he that seeketh findeth; and to him that knocketh it shall be opened."
> MATTHEW 7:8

PRAYER JOURNAL
Day 8

DATE _____

S M T W T F S

PRAYER REQUESTS

- _____
- _____
- _____
- _____
- _____
- _____

SCRIPTURE REFERENCES

_____
_____
_____
_____
_____
_____

GOD'S RESPONSE

_____
_____
_____
_____
_____
_____

> Therefore I say unto you, What things soever ye desire, when ye pray, believe that ye receive them, and ye shall have them.
> MARK 11:24 KJV

Stones of Remembrance

DATE _____

S M T W T F S

ANSWERED PRAYER

REMEMBRANCE

_____
_____
_____
_____

ANSWERED PRAYER

REMEMBRANCE

_____
_____
_____
_____

> And if we know that he hear us, whatsoever we ask, we know that we have the petitions that we desired of him.
>
> 1 JOHN 5:15

PRAYER JOURNAL
Day 9

DATE _____

S M T W T F S

PRAYER REQUESTS

- _____
- _____
- _____

- _____
- _____
- _____

SCRIPTURE REFERENCES

_____
_____
_____
_____
_____

GOD'S RESPONSE

_____
_____
_____
_____

> " Be careful for nothing; but in every thing by prayer and supplication with thanksgiving let your requests be made known unto God. And the peace of God, which passeth all understanding, shall keep your hearts and minds through Christ Jesus.
>
> **PHILIPPIANS 4:6-7** "

DATE

S M T W T F S

ANSWERED PRAYER

REMEMBRANCE

ANSWERED PRAYER

REMEMBRANCE

> But verily God hath heard me; he hath attended to the voice of my prayer. Blessed be God, which hath not turned away my prayer, nor his mercy from me.
>
> PSALM 66:19-20

PRAYER JOURNAL
Day 10

DATE

S M T W T F S

PRAYER REQUESTS

- _____
- _____
- _____

- _____
- _____
- _____

SCRIPTURE REFERENCES

_____
_____
_____
_____
_____
_____

GOD'S RESPONSE

_____
_____
_____
_____
_____
_____

> *Call unto me, and I will answer thee, and show thee great and mighty things, which thou knowest not.*
> **JEREMIAH 33:3**

Stones of Remembrance

DATE _____

S M T W T F S

ANSWERED PRAYER

REMEMBRANCE

_____
_____
_____
_____

ANSWERED PRAYER

REMEMBRANCE

_____
_____
_____
_____

> For the eyes of the Lord are over the righteous, and his ears are open unto their prayers: but the face of the Lord is against them that do evil.
> **1 PETER 3:12**

PRAYER JOURNAL
Day 11

DATE _____

S M T W T F S

PRAYER REQUESTS

- _____
- _____
- _____

- _____
- _____
- _____

SCRIPTURE REFERENCES

_____
_____
_____
_____
_____
_____

GOD'S RESPONSE

_____
_____
_____
_____
_____
_____

> *And all things, whatsoever ye shall ask in prayer, believing, ye shall receive.*
> **MATTHEW 21:22**

Stones of Remembrance

DATE _____

S M T W T F S

ANSWERED PRAYER

```
[                                              ]
```

REMEMBRANCE

_____
_____
_____
_____

ANSWERED PRAYER

```
[                                              ]
```

REMEMBRANCE

_____
_____
_____
_____

> The righteous cry, and the LORD heareth, and delivereth them out of all their troubles.
>
> PSALM 34:17

PRAYER JOURNAL
Day 12

DATE

S M T W T F S

PRAYER REQUESTS

- _____
- _____
- _____
- _____
- _____

SCRIPTURE REFERENCES

_____
_____
_____
_____
_____
_____

GOD'S RESPONSE

_____
_____
_____
_____
_____
_____

> *And whatsoever we ask, we receive of him, because we keep his commandments, and do those things that are pleasing in his sight.*
> **1 JOHN 3:22**

DATE _____

S M T W T F S

ANSWERED PRAYER

REMEMBRANCE

ANSWERED PRAYER

REMEMBRANCE

O thou that hearest prayer, unto thee shall all flesh come.
PSALM 65:2

PRAYER JOURNAL
Day 13

DATE

S M T W T F S

PRAYER REQUESTS

- _____
- _____
- _____
- _____
- _____
- _____

SCRIPTURE REFERENCES

_____
_____
_____
_____
_____
_____

GOD'S RESPONSE

_____
_____
_____
_____
_____
_____

> " If ye shall ask any thing in my name, I will do it.
> JOHN 14:14 "

DATE

S M T W T F S

ANSWERED PRAYER

REMEMBRANCE

ANSWERED PRAYER

REMEMBRANCE

Then shall ye call upon me, and ye shall go and pray unto me, and I will hearken unto you.
JEREMIAH 29:12

PRAYER JOURNAL
Day 14

DATE _____

S M T W T F S

PRAYER REQUESTS

- _____
- _____
- _____
- _____
- _____
- _____

SCRIPTURE REFERENCES

_____
_____
_____
_____
_____
_____

GOD'S RESPONSE

_____
_____
_____
_____
_____
_____

> Ask, and it shall be given you; seek, and ye shall find; knock, and it shall be opened unto you
> MATTHEW 7:7

DATE

S M T W T F S

ANSWERED PRAYER

REMEMBRANCE

_____
_____
_____
_____

ANSWERED PRAYER

REMEMBRANCE

_____
_____
_____
_____

> "For every one that asketh receiveth; and he that seeketh findeth; and to him that knocketh it shall be opened.
> MATTHEW 7:8

PRAYER JOURNAL
Day 15

DATE _____

S M T W T F S

PRAYER REQUESTS

- _____
- _____
- _____
- _____
- _____

SCRIPTURE REFERENCES

_____
_____
_____
_____
_____
_____

GOD'S RESPONSE

_____
_____
_____
_____
_____
_____

Therefore I say unto you, What things soever ye desire, when ye pray, believe that ye receive them, and ye shall have them.
MARK 11:24 KJV

Stones of Remembrance

DATE _____

S M T W T F S

ANSWERED PRAYER

REMEMBRANCE

ANSWERED PRAYER

REMEMBRANCE

And if we know that he hear us, whatsoever we ask, we know that we have the petitions that we desired of him.
1 JOHN 5:15

PRAYER JOURNAL
Day 16

DATE _____

S M T W T F S

PRAYER REQUESTS

- _____
- _____
- _____
- _____
- _____
- _____

SCRIPTURE REFERENCES

_____
_____
_____
_____
_____
_____

GOD'S RESPONSE

_____
_____
_____
_____

> " Be careful for nothing; but in every thing by prayer and supplication with thanksgiving let your requests be made known unto God. And the peace of God, which passeth all understanding, shall keep your hearts and minds through Christ Jesus.
>
> **PHILIPPIANS 4:6-7** "

DATE _____

S M T W T F S

ANSWERED PRAYER

REMEMBRANCE

ANSWERED PRAYER

REMEMBRANCE

> " But verily God hath heard me; he hath attended to the voice of my prayer. Blessed be God, which hath not turned away my prayer, nor his mercy from me.
>
> PSALM 66:19-20 "

PRAYER JOURNAL
Day 17

DATE
_____

S   M   T   W   T   F   S

PRAYER REQUESTS

- _____
- _____
- _____

- _____
- _____
- _____

SCRIPTURE REFERENCES

_____
_____
_____
_____
_____
_____

GOD'S RESPONSE

_____
_____
_____
_____
_____
_____

> *Call unto me, and I will answer thee, and show thee great and mighty things, which thou knowest not.*
> **JEREMIAH 33:3**

DATE _____

S M T W T F S

ANSWERED PRAYER

REMEMBRANCE

ANSWERED PRAYER

REMEMBRANCE

 For the eyes of the Lord are over the righteous, and his ears are open unto their prayers: but the face of the Lord is against them that do evil.

1 PETER 3:12

PRAYER JOURNAL
Day 18

DATE

S M T W T F S

PRAYER REQUESTS

-
-
-
-
-
-

SCRIPTURE REFERENCES

GOD'S RESPONSE

And all things, whatsoever ye shall ask in prayer, believing, ye shall receive.
MATTHEW 21:22

DATE _____

S M T W T F S

ANSWERED PRAYER

REMEMBRANCE

ANSWERED PRAYER

REMEMBRANCE

 The righteous cry, and the LORD heareth, and delivereth them out of all their troubles.
PSALM 34:17

PRAYER JOURNAL
Day 19

DATE

S M T W T F S

PRAYER REQUESTS

-
-
-
-
-
-

SCRIPTURE REFERENCES

_____
_____
_____
_____
_____
_____

GOD'S RESPONSE

_____
_____
_____
_____
_____
_____

> "And whatsoever we ask, we receive of him, because we keep his commandments, and do those things that are pleasing in his sight."
> 1 JOHN 3:22

DATE _____

S M T W T F S

ANSWERED PRAYER

REMEMBRANCE

_____
_____
_____
_____

ANSWERED PRAYER

REMEMBRANCE

_____
_____
_____
_____

 O thou that hearest prayer, unto thee shall all flesh come.

PSALM 65:2

PRAYER JOURNAL
Day 20

DATE

S M T W T F S

PRAYER REQUESTS

-
-
-
-
-
-

SCRIPTURE REFERENCES

_____
_____
_____
_____
_____
_____

GOD'S RESPONSE

_____
_____
_____
_____
_____
_____

> " If ye shall ask any thing in my name, I will do it.
> JOHN 14:14 "

DATE _____

S M T W T F S

ANSWERED PRAYER

REMEMBRANCE

_____
_____
_____
_____

ANSWERED PRAYER

REMEMBRANCE

_____
_____
_____
_____

 Then shall ye call upon me, and ye shall go and pray unto me, and I will hearken unto you.
JEREMIAH 29:12

PRAYER JOURNAL
Day 21

DATE _____

S M T W T F S

PRAYER REQUESTS

- _____
- _____
- _____
- _____
- _____
- _____

SCRIPTURE REFERENCES

_____
_____
_____
_____
_____
_____

GOD'S RESPONSE

_____
_____
_____
_____
_____
_____

> *Ask, and it shall be given you; seek, and ye shall find; knock, and it shall be opened unto you*
> MATTHEW 7:7

DATE
S M T W T F S

ANSWERED PRAYER

REMEMBRANCE

ANSWERED PRAYER

REMEMBRANCE

> "For every one that asketh receiveth; and he that seeketh findeth; and to him that knocketh it shall be opened.
> MATTHEW 7:8"

PRAYER JOURNAL
Day 22

DATE

S M T W T F S

PRAYER REQUESTS

-
-
-
-
-
-

SCRIPTURE REFERENCES

GOD'S RESPONSE

 Therefore I say unto you, What things soever ye desire, when ye pray, believe that ye receive them, and ye shall have them.
MARK 11:24 KJV

Stones of Remembrance

DATE _____

S M T W T F S

ANSWERED PRAYER

REMEMBRANCE

ANSWERED PRAYER

REMEMBRANCE

 And if we know that he hear us, whatsoever we ask, we know that we have the petitions that we desired of him.
1 JOHN 5:15

PRAYER JOURNAL
Day 23

DATE

S M T W T F S

PRAYER REQUESTS

-
-
-
-
-
-

SCRIPTURE REFERENCES

_____
_____
_____
_____
_____
_____

GOD'S RESPONSE

_____
_____
_____
_____

> "Be careful for nothing; but in every thing by prayer and supplication with thanksgiving let your requests be made known unto God. And the peace of God, which passeth all understanding, shall keep your hearts and minds through Christ Jesus."
>
> PHILIPPIANS 4:6-7

DATE

S M T W T F S

ANSWERED PRAYER

REMEMBRANCE

___

ANSWERED PRAYER

REMEMBRANCE

___

> " But verily God hath heard me; he hath attended to the voice of my prayer. Blessed be God, which hath not turned away my prayer, nor his mercy from me.
>
> PSALM 66:19-20 "

PRAYER JOURNAL
Day 24

DATE _____

S M T W T F S

PRAYER REQUESTS

- _____
- _____
- _____
- _____
- _____
- _____

SCRIPTURE REFERENCES

_____
_____
_____
_____
_____
_____

GOD'S RESPONSE

_____
_____
_____
_____
_____
_____

Call unto me, and I will answer thee, and show thee great and mighty things, which thou knowest not.

JEREMIAH 33:3

DATE

S M T W T F S

ANSWERED PRAYER

REMEMBRANCE

ANSWERED PRAYER

REMEMBRANCE

 For the eyes of the Lord are over the righteous, and his ears are open unto their prayers: but the face of the Lord is against them that do evil.
1 PETER 3:12

PRAYER JOURNAL
Day 25

DATE _____

S M T W T F S
○ ○ ○ ○ ○ ○ ○

PRAYER REQUESTS

- _____
- _____
- _____

- _____
- _____
- _____

SCRIPTURE REFERENCES

_____
_____
_____
_____
_____
_____

GOD'S RESPONSE

_____
_____
_____
_____
_____
_____

And all things, whatsoever ye shall ask in prayer, believing, ye shall receive.
MATTHEW 21:22

Stones of Remembrance

DATE _____

S M T W T F S

ANSWERED PRAYER

REMEMBRANCE

ANSWERED PRAYER

REMEMBRANCE

> The righteous cry, and the LORD heareth, and delivereth them out of all their troubles.
>
> **PSALM 34:17**

PRAYER JOURNAL
Day 26

DATE _____

S M T W T F S

PRAYER REQUESTS

- _____
- _____
- _____
- _____
- _____
- _____

SCRIPTURE REFERENCES

_____
_____
_____
_____
_____
_____

GOD'S RESPONSE

_____
_____
_____
_____
_____
_____

> And whatsoever we ask, we receive of him, because we keep his commandments, and do those things that are pleasing in his sight.
> **1 JOHN 3:22**

DATE _____

S M T W T F S

ANSWERED PRAYER

REMEMBRANCE

ANSWERED PRAYER

REMEMBRANCE

 O thou that hearest prayer, unto thee shall all flesh come.
PSALM 65:2

PRAYER JOURNAL
Day 27

DATE _____

S M T W T F S

PRAYER REQUESTS

- _____
- _____
- _____
- _____
- _____
- _____

SCRIPTURE REFERENCES

_____
_____
_____
_____
_____
_____

GOD'S RESPONSE

_____
_____
_____
_____
_____
_____

If ye shall ask any thing in my name, I will do it.

JOHN 14:14

Stones of Remembrance

DATE _____

S M T W T F S

ANSWERED PRAYER

REMEMBRANCE

_____
_____
_____
_____

ANSWERED PRAYER

REMEMBRANCE

_____
_____
_____
_____

> Then shall ye call upon me, and ye shall go and pray unto me, and I will hearken unto you.
> **JEREMIAH 29:12**

PRAYER JOURNAL
Day 28

DATE
_____

S M T W T F S

PRAYER REQUESTS

- _____
- _____
- _____

- _____
- _____
- _____

SCRIPTURE REFERENCES

_____
_____
_____
_____
_____
_____

GOD'S RESPONSE

_____
_____
_____
_____
_____
_____

> *Ask, and it shall be given you; seek, and ye shall find; knock, and it shall be opened unto you*
> **MATTHEW 7:7**

Stones of Remembrance

DATE _____

S M T W T F S

ANSWERED PRAYER

REMEMBRANCE

ANSWERED PRAYER

REMEMBRANCE

 For every one that asketh receiveth; and he that seeketh findeth; and to him that knocketh it shall be opened.
MATTHEW 7:8

PRAYER JOURNAL
Day 29

DATE _____

S M T W T F S

PRAYER REQUESTS

- _____
- _____
- _____
- _____
- _____
- _____

SCRIPTURE REFERENCES

_____
_____
_____
_____
_____
_____

GOD'S RESPONSE

_____
_____
_____
_____
_____
_____
_____

> Therefore I say unto you, What things soever ye desire, when ye pray, believe that ye receive them, and ye shall have them.
>
> **MARK 11:24 KJV**

DATE _____

S M T W T F S

ANSWERED PRAYER

REMEMBRANCE

_____
_____
_____
_____

ANSWERED PRAYER

REMEMBRANCE

_____
_____
_____
_____

 And if we know that he hear us, whatsoever we ask, we know that we have the petitions that we desired of him.
1 JOHN 5:15

PRAYER JOURNAL
Day 30

DATE _____

S M T W T F S

PRAYER REQUESTS

- _____
- _____
- _____
- _____
- _____
- _____

SCRIPTURE REFERENCES

_____
_____
_____
_____
_____
_____

GOD'S RESPONSE

_____
_____
_____
_____
_____

> "Be careful for nothing; but in every thing by prayer and supplication with thanksgiving let your requests be made known unto God. And the peace of God, which passeth all understanding, shall keep your hearts and minds through Christ Jesus."
>
> **PHILIPPIANS 4:6-7**

DATE _____

S M T W T F S

ANSWERED PRAYER

REMEMBRANCE

ANSWERED PRAYER

REMEMBRANCE

> " But verily God hath heard me; he hath attended to the voice of my prayer.
> Blessed be God, which hath not turned away my prayer,
> nor his mercy from me.
>
> PSALM 66:19-20 "

PRAYER JOURNAL
Day 31

DATE

S M T W T F S

PRAYER REQUESTS

- _____
- _____
- _____
- _____
- _____
- _____

SCRIPTURE REFERENCES

_____
_____
_____
_____
_____
_____

GOD'S RESPONSE

_____
_____
_____
_____
_____
_____

Call unto me, and I will answer thee, and show thee great and mighty things, which thou knowest not.
JEREMIAH 33:3

DATE _____

S M T W T F S

ANSWERED PRAYER

REMEMBRANCE

ANSWERED PRAYER

REMEMBRANCE

 For the eyes of the Lord are over the righteous, and his ears are open unto their prayers: but the face of the Lord is against them that do evil.
1 PETER 3:12

PRAYER JOURNAL
Day 32

DATE

S M T W T F S

PRAYER REQUESTS

- _____
- _____
- _____
- _____
- _____
- _____

SCRIPTURE REFERENCES

_____
_____
_____
_____
_____
_____

GOD'S RESPONSE

_____
_____
_____
_____
_____
_____

 And all things, whatsoever ye shall ask in prayer, believing, ye shall receive.
MATTHEW 21:22

DATE _____

S M T W T F S

ANSWERED PRAYER

REMEMBRANCE

_____
_____
_____
_____
_____

ANSWERED PRAYER

REMEMBRANCE

_____
_____
_____
_____
_____

 The righteous cry, and the LORD heareth, and delivereth them out of all their troubles.
PSALM 34:17

PRAYER JOURNAL
Day 33

DATE _____

S M T W T F S

PRAYER REQUESTS

- _____
- _____
- _____
- _____
- _____
- _____

SCRIPTURE REFERENCES

_____
_____
_____
_____
_____
_____

GOD'S RESPONSE

_____
_____
_____
_____
_____
_____

> And whatsoever we ask, we receive of him, because we keep his commandments, and do those things that are pleasing in his sight.
> 1 JOHN 3:22

DATE

S M T W T F S

ANSWERED PRAYER

REMEMBRANCE

ANSWERED PRAYER

REMEMBRANCE

> "O thou that hearest prayer, unto thee shall all flesh come."
> PSALM 65:2

PRAYER JOURNAL
Day 34

DATE

S M T W T F S

PRAYER REQUESTS

-
-
-
-
-
-

SCRIPTURE REFERENCES

GOD'S RESPONSE

> If ye shall ask any thing in my name, I will do it.
> JOHN 14:14

DATE _____

S M T W T F S

ANSWERED PRAYER

REMEMBRANCE

___

ANSWERED PRAYER

REMEMBRANCE

 Then shall ye call upon me, and ye shall go and pray unto me, and I will hearken unto you.
JEREMIAH 29:12

PRAYER JOURNAL
Day 35

DATE _____

S M T W T F S

PRAYER REQUESTS

- _____
- _____
- _____
- _____
- _____
- _____

SCRIPTURE REFERENCES

_____
_____
_____
_____
_____
_____

GOD'S RESPONSE

_____
_____
_____
_____
_____
_____

Ask, and it shall be given you; seek, and ye shall find; knock, and it shall be opened unto you
MATTHEW 7:7

Stones of Remembrance

DATE _____

S M T W T F S

ANSWERED PRAYER

REMEMBRANCE

_____
_____
_____
_____

ANSWERED PRAYER

REMEMBRANCE

_____
_____
_____
_____

> "For every one that asketh receiveth; and he that seeketh findeth; and to him that knocketh it shall be opened."
> MATTHEW 7:8

PRAYER JOURNAL
Day 36

DATE _____

S M T W T F S

PRAYER REQUESTS

- _____
- _____
- _____
- _____
- _____
- _____

SCRIPTURE REFERENCES

_____
_____
_____
_____
_____
_____

GOD'S RESPONSE

_____
_____
_____
_____
_____
_____

> Therefore I say unto you, What things soever ye desire, when ye pray, believe that ye receive them, and ye shall have them.
> MARK 11:24 KJV

Stones of Remembrance

DATE _____

S M T W T F S

ANSWERED PRAYER

REMEMBRANCE

_____
_____
_____
_____

ANSWERED PRAYER

REMEMBRANCE

_____
_____
_____
_____

 And if we know that he hear us, whatsoever we ask, we know that we have the petitions that we desired of him.

1 JOHN 5:15

PRAYER JOURNAL
Day 37

DATE

S M T W T F S

PRAYER REQUESTS

- _____
- _____
- _____
- _____
- _____
- _____

SCRIPTURE REFERENCES

_____
_____
_____
_____
_____
_____

GOD'S RESPONSE

_____
_____
_____
_____

> " *Be careful for nothing; but in every thing by prayer and supplication with thanksgiving let your requests be made known unto God. And the peace of God, which passeth all understanding, shall keep your hearts and minds through Christ Jesus.*
>
> PHILIPPIANS 4:6-7 "

DATE _____

S M T W T F S

ANSWERED PRAYER

REMEMBRANCE

_____
_____
_____

ANSWERED PRAYER

REMEMBRANCE

_____
_____
_____

> "But verily God hath heard me; he hath attended to the voice of my prayer. Blessed be God, which hath not turned away my prayer, nor his mercy from me.
>
> PSALM 66:19-20"

PRAYER JOURNAL
Day 38

DATE _____

S M T W T F S

PRAYER REQUESTS

- _____
- _____
- _____
- _____
- _____
- _____

SCRIPTURE REFERENCES

_____
_____
_____
_____
_____
_____

GOD'S RESPONSE

_____
_____
_____
_____
_____
_____
_____

Call unto me, and I will answer thee, and show thee great and mighty things, which thou knowest not.

JEREMIAH 33:3

Stones of Remembrance

DATE _____

S M T W T F S

ANSWERED PRAYER

REMEMBRANCE

ANSWERED PRAYER

REMEMBRANCE

 For the eyes of the Lord are over the righteous, and his ears are open unto their prayers: but the face of the Lord is against them that do evil.
1 PETER 3:12

PRAYER JOURNAL
Day 39

DATE

S M T W T F S

PRAYER REQUESTS

- _____
- _____
- _____
- _____
- _____
- _____

SCRIPTURE REFERENCES

_____
_____
_____
_____
_____
_____

GOD'S RESPONSE

_____
_____
_____
_____
_____
_____

> And all things, whatsoever ye shall ask in prayer, believing, ye shall receive.
> MATTHEW 21:22

DATE _____

S M T W T F S

ANSWERED PRAYER

REMEMBRANCE

_____
_____
_____
_____
_____

ANSWERED PRAYER

REMEMBRANCE

_____
_____
_____
_____
_____

 The righteous cry, and the LORD heareth, and delivereth them out of all their troubles.
PSALM 34:17

PRAYER JOURNAL
Day 40

DATE _____

S M T W T F S

PRAYER REQUESTS

- _____
- _____
- _____
- _____
- _____
- _____

SCRIPTURE REFERENCES

_____
_____
_____
_____
_____
_____

GOD'S RESPONSE

_____
_____
_____
_____
_____
_____

> And whatsoever we ask, we receive of him, because we keep his commandments, and do those things that are pleasing in his sight.
> 1 JOHN 3:22

DATE

S M T W T F S

ANSWERED PRAYER

REMEMBRANCE

___

ANSWERED PRAYER

REMEMBRANCE

> "O thou that hearest prayer, unto thee shall all flesh come.
> PSALM 65:2"

PRAYER JOURNAL
Day 41

DATE _____

S M T W T F S

PRAYER REQUESTS

- _____
- _____
- _____
- _____
- _____
- _____

SCRIPTURE REFERENCES

_____
_____
_____
_____
_____
_____

GOD'S RESPONSE

_____
_____
_____
_____
_____
_____

> If ye shall ask any thing in my name, I will do it.
>
> JOHN 14:14

DATE _____

S M T W T F S

ANSWERED PRAYER

REMEMBRANCE

_____
_____
_____
_____

ANSWERED PRAYER

REMEMBRANCE

_____
_____
_____
_____

 Then shall ye call upon me, and ye shall go and pray unto me, and I will hearken unto you.
JEREMIAH 29:12

PRAYER JOURNAL
Day 42

DATE _____

S M T W T F S

PRAYER REQUESTS

- _____
- _____
- _____
- _____
- _____
- _____

SCRIPTURE REFERENCES

_____
_____
_____
_____
_____
_____

GOD'S RESPONSE

_____
_____
_____
_____
_____
_____

Ask, and it shall be given you; seek, and ye shall find; knock, and it shall be opened unto you
MATTHEW 7:7

DATE _____

S M T W T F S

ANSWERED PRAYER

REMEMBRANCE

_____
_____
_____
_____

ANSWERED PRAYER

REMEMBRANCE

_____
_____
_____
_____

> " For every one that asketh receiveth; and he that seeketh findeth; and to him that knocketh it shall be opened.
> MATTHEW 7:8 "

PRAYER JOURNAL
Day 43

DATE

S M T W T F S

PRAYER REQUESTS

-
-
-
-
-
-

SCRIPTURE REFERENCES

_____
_____
_____
_____
_____
_____

GOD'S RESPONSE

_____
_____
_____
_____
_____
_____

> Therefore I say unto you, What things soever ye desire, when ye pray, believe that ye receive them, and ye shall have them.
>
> MARK 11:24 KJV

DATE _____

S M T W T F S

ANSWERED PRAYER

REMEMBRANCE

_____
_____
_____
_____

ANSWERED PRAYER

REMEMBRANCE

_____
_____
_____
_____

> And if we know that he hear us, whatsoever we ask, we know that we have the petitions that we desired of him.
> 1 JOHN 5:15

PRAYER JOURNAL
Day 44

DATE _____

S M T W T F S

PRAYER REQUESTS

- _____
- _____
- _____
- _____
- _____
- _____

SCRIPTURE REFERENCES

_____
_____
_____
_____
_____
_____

GOD'S RESPONSE

_____
_____
_____
_____

> *Be careful for nothing; but in every thing by prayer and supplication with thanksgiving let your requests be made known unto God. And the peace of God, which passeth all understanding, shall keep your hearts and minds through Christ Jesus.*
>
> **PHILIPPIANS 4:6-7**

DATE

S M T W T F S

ANSWERED PRAYER

REMEMBRANCE

___

ANSWERED PRAYER

REMEMBRANCE

___

> " But verily God hath heard me; he hath attended to the voice of my prayer. Blessed be God, which hath not turned away my prayer, nor his mercy from me.
>
> PSALM 66:19-20 "

PRAYER JOURNAL
Day 45

DATE _____

S M T W T F S

PRAYER REQUESTS

- _____
- _____
- _____

- _____
- _____
- _____

SCRIPTURE REFERENCES

_____
_____
_____
_____
_____
_____

GOD'S RESPONSE

_____
_____
_____
_____
_____
_____

> Call unto me, and I will answer thee, and show thee great and mighty things, which thou knowest not.
> **JEREMIAH 33:3**

DATE _____

S M T W T F S

ANSWERED PRAYER

REMEMBRANCE

_____
_____
_____
_____

ANSWERED PRAYER

REMEMBRANCE

_____
_____
_____
_____

 For the eyes of the Lord are over the righteous, and his ears are open unto their prayers: but the face of the Lord is against them that do evil.
1 PETER 3:12

PRAYER JOURNAL
Day 46

DATE

S M T W T F S

PRAYER REQUESTS

- _____
- _____
- _____
- _____
- _____
- _____

SCRIPTURE REFERENCES

_____
_____
_____
_____
_____
_____

GOD'S RESPONSE

_____
_____
_____
_____
_____
_____

> And all things, whatsoever ye shall ask in prayer, believing, ye shall receive.
> MATTHEW 21:22

DATE _____

S M T W T F S

ANSWERED PRAYER

REMEMBRANCE

_____
_____
_____
_____

ANSWERED PRAYER

REMEMBRANCE

_____
_____
_____
_____

 The righteous cry, and the LORD heareth, and delivereth them out of all their troubles.
PSALM 34:17

PRAYER JOURNAL
Day 47

DATE _____

S M T W T F S

PRAYER REQUESTS

- _____
- _____
- _____
- _____
- _____
- _____

SCRIPTURE REFERENCES

_____
_____
_____
_____
_____
_____

GOD'S RESPONSE

_____
_____
_____
_____
_____
_____

> And whatsoever we ask, we receive of him, because we keep his commandments, and do those things that are pleasing in his sight.
> 1 JOHN 3:22

DATE

S M T W T F S

ANSWERED PRAYER

REMEMBRANCE

_____
_____
_____
_____

ANSWERED PRAYER

REMEMBRANCE

_____
_____
_____
_____

> " O thou that hearest prayer, unto thee shall all flesh come.
> PSALM 65:2 "

PRAYER JOURNAL
Day 48

DATE

S M T W T F S

PRAYER REQUESTS

- _____
- _____
- _____
- _____
- _____
- _____

SCRIPTURE REFERENCES

_____
_____
_____
_____
_____
_____

GOD'S RESPONSE

_____
_____
_____
_____
_____
_____

> If ye shall ask any thing in my name, I will do it.
> JOHN 14:14

Stones of Remembrance

DATE _____

S M T W T F S

ANSWERED PRAYER

REMEMBRANCE

_____
_____
_____
_____

ANSWERED PRAYER

REMEMBRANCE

_____
_____
_____
_____

 Then shall ye call upon me, and ye shall go and pray unto me, and I will hearken unto you.

JEREMIAH 29:12

PRAYER JOURNAL
Day 49

DATE _____

S M T W T F S

PRAYER REQUESTS

- _____
- _____
- _____
- _____
- _____
- _____

SCRIPTURE REFERENCES

_____
_____
_____
_____
_____
_____

GOD'S RESPONSE

_____
_____
_____
_____
_____
_____

> *Ask, and it shall be given you; seek, and ye shall find; knock, and it shall be opened unto you*
> **MATTHEW 7:7**

Stones of Remembrance

DATE _____

S M T W T F S

ANSWERED PRAYER

REMEMBRANCE

ANSWERED PRAYER

REMEMBRANCE

> "For every one that asketh receiveth; and he that seeketh findeth; and to him that knocketh it shall be opened.
> MATTHEW 7:8

PRAYER JOURNAL
Day 50

DATE

S M T W T F S

PRAYER REQUESTS

- _____
- _____
- _____
- _____
- _____
- _____

SCRIPTURE REFERENCES

_____
_____
_____
_____
_____
_____

GOD'S RESPONSE

_____
_____
_____
_____
_____
_____

> Therefore I say unto you, What things soever ye desire, when ye pray, believe that ye receive them, and ye shall have them.
> MARK 11:24 KJV

DATE _____

S M T W T F S

ANSWERED PRAYER

REMEMBRANCE

_____
_____
_____
_____

ANSWERED PRAYER

REMEMBRANCE

_____
_____
_____
_____

> And if we know that he hear us, whatsoever we ask, we know that we have the petitions that we desired of him.
> **1 JOHN 5:15**

PRAYER JOURNAL
Day 51

DATE _____

S M T W T F S

PRAYER REQUESTS

- _____
- _____
- _____
- _____
- _____
- _____

SCRIPTURE REFERENCES

_____
_____
_____
_____
_____
_____

GOD'S RESPONSE

_____
_____
_____
_____
_____

> " Be careful for nothing; but in every thing by prayer and supplication with thanksgiving let your requests be made known unto God. And the peace of God, which passeth all understanding, shall keep your hearts and minds through Christ Jesus.
>
> PHILIPPIANS 4:6-7 "

DATE ____

S M T W T F S

ANSWERED PRAYER

REMEMBRANCE

ANSWERED PRAYER

REMEMBRANCE

> "But verily God hath heard me; he hath attended to the voice of my prayer. Blessed be God, which hath not turned away my prayer, nor his mercy from me.
>
> PSALM 66:19-20

PRAYER JOURNAL
Day 52

DATE _____

S M T W T F S

PRAYER REQUESTS

- _____
- _____
- _____
- _____
- _____
- _____

SCRIPTURE REFERENCES

_____
_____
_____
_____
_____
_____

GOD'S RESPONSE

_____
_____
_____
_____
_____
_____

> *Call unto me, and I will answer thee, and show thee great and mighty things, which thou knowest not.*
> **JEREMIAH 33:3**

DATE _____

S M T W T F S

ANSWERED PRAYER

REMEMBRANCE

_____
_____
_____
_____

ANSWERED PRAYER

REMEMBRANCE

_____
_____
_____
_____

For the eyes of the Lord are over the righteous, and his ears are open unto their prayers: but the face of the Lord is against them that do evil.
1 PETER 3:12

PRAYER JOURNAL
Day 53

DATE

S M T W T F S

PRAYER REQUESTS

-
-
-
-
-
-

SCRIPTURE REFERENCES

GOD'S RESPONSE

And all things, whatsoever ye shall ask in prayer, believing, ye shall receive.
MATTHEW 21:22

Stones of Remembrance

DATE _____

S M T W T F S

ANSWERED PRAYER

REMEMBRANCE

ANSWERED PRAYER

REMEMBRANCE

 The righteous cry, and the LORD heareth, and delivereth them out of all their troubles.
PSALM 34:17

PRAYER JOURNAL
Day 54

DATE _____

S M T W T F S

PRAYER REQUESTS

- _____
- _____
- _____
- _____
- _____
- _____

SCRIPTURE REFERENCES

_____
_____
_____
_____
_____
_____

GOD'S RESPONSE

_____
_____
_____
_____
_____
_____

> And whatsoever we ask, we receive of him, because we keep his commandments, and do those things that are pleasing in his sight.
> 1 JOHN 3:22

DATE _____

S M T W T F S

ANSWERED PRAYER

REMEMBRANCE

_____
_____
_____
_____

ANSWERED PRAYER

REMEMBRANCE

_____
_____
_____
_____

 O thou that hearest prayer, unto thee shall all flesh come.

PSALM 65:2

PRAYER JOURNAL
Day 55

DATE

S M T W T F S

PRAYER REQUESTS

-
-
-
-
-
-

SCRIPTURE REFERENCES

GOD'S RESPONSE

If ye shall ask any thing in my name, I will do it.
JOHN 14:14

Stones of Remembrance

DATE _____

S M T W T F S

ANSWERED PRAYER

REMEMBRANCE

ANSWERED PRAYER

REMEMBRANCE

 Then shall ye call upon me, and ye shall go and pray unto me, and I will hearken unto you.
JEREMIAH 29:12

PRAYER JOURNAL
Day 56

DATE

S M T W T F S

PRAYER REQUESTS

- _____
- _____
- _____
- _____
- _____
- _____

SCRIPTURE REFERENCES

_____
_____
_____
_____
_____
_____

GOD'S RESPONSE

_____
_____
_____
_____
_____
_____

> Ask, and it shall be given you; seek, and ye shall find; knock, and it shall be opened unto you
> MATTHEW 7:7

DATE

S M T W T F S

ANSWERED PRAYER

REMEMBRANCE

_____
_____
_____
_____

ANSWERED PRAYER

REMEMBRANCE

_____
_____
_____
_____

> "For every one that asketh receiveth; and he that seeketh findeth; and to him that knocketh it shall be opened.
> MATTHEW 7:8"

PRAYER JOURNAL
Day 57

DATE _____

S M T W T F S

PRAYER REQUESTS

- _____
- _____
- _____
- _____
- _____
- _____

SCRIPTURE REFERENCES

_____
_____
_____
_____
_____
_____

GOD'S RESPONSE

_____
_____
_____
_____
_____
_____

 Therefore I say unto you, What things soever ye desire, when ye pray, believe that ye receive them, and ye shall have them.
MARK 11:24 KJV

DATE
S M T W T F S

ANSWERED PRAYER

REMEMBRANCE

_____
_____
_____
_____
_____

ANSWERED PRAYER

REMEMBRANCE

_____
_____
_____
_____
_____

" And if we know that he hear us, whatsoever we ask, we know that we have the petitions that we desired of him.
1 JOHN 5:15 "

PRAYER JOURNAL
Day 58

DATE

S M T W T F S

PRAYER REQUESTS

-
-
-
-
-
-

SCRIPTURE REFERENCES

GOD'S RESPONSE

> " Be careful for nothing; but in every thing by prayer and supplication with thanksgiving let your requests be made known unto God. And the peace of God, which passeth all understanding, shall keep your hearts and minds through Christ Jesus.
>
> **PHILIPPIANS 4:6-7** "

DATE

S M T W T F S

ANSWERED PRAYER

REMEMBRANCE

ANSWERED PRAYER

REMEMBRANCE

> But verily God hath heard me; he hath attended to the voice of my prayer. Blessed be God, which hath not turned away my prayer, nor his mercy from me.
>
> PSALM 66:19-20

PRAYER JOURNAL
Day 59

DATE

S M T W T F S

PRAYER REQUESTS

- _____
- _____
- _____
- _____
- _____
- _____

SCRIPTURE REFERENCES

_____
_____
_____
_____
_____
_____

GOD'S RESPONSE

_____
_____
_____
_____
_____
_____
_____

Call unto me, and I will answer thee, and show thee great and mighty things, which thou knowest not.

JEREMIAH 33:3

DATE

S M T W T F S

ANSWERED PRAYER

REMEMBRANCE

ANSWERED PRAYER

REMEMBRANCE

 For the eyes of the Lord are over the righteous, and his ears are open unto their prayers: but the face of the Lord is against them that do evil.
1 PETER 3:12

PRAYER JOURNAL
Day 60

DATE _____

S M T W T F S

PRAYER REQUESTS

- _____
- _____
- _____
- _____
- _____
- _____

SCRIPTURE REFERENCES

_____
_____
_____
_____
_____
_____

GOD'S RESPONSE

_____
_____
_____
_____
_____
_____
_____

> And all things, whatsoever ye shall ask in prayer, believing, ye shall receive.
> MATTHEW 21:22

DATE _____

S M T W T F S
• • • • • • •

ANSWERED PRAYER

REMEMBRANCE

_____
_____
_____
_____

ANSWERED PRAYER

REMEMBRANCE

_____
_____
_____
_____

> The righteous cry, and the LORD heareth, and delivereth them out of all their troubles.
> PSALM 34:17

PRAYER JOURNAL
Day 61

DATE

S M T W T F S

PRAYER REQUESTS

-
-
-
-
-
-

SCRIPTURE REFERENCES

_____
_____
_____
_____
_____
_____

GOD'S RESPONSE

_____
_____
_____
_____
_____
_____

> And whatsoever we ask, we receive of him, because we keep his commandments, and do those things that are pleasing in his sight.
> 1 JOHN 3:22

DATE _____

S M T W T F S

ANSWERED PRAYER

REMEMBRANCE

ANSWERED PRAYER

REMEMBRANCE

 O thou that hearest prayer, unto thee shall all flesh come.

PSALM 65:2

PRAYER JOURNAL
Day 62

DATE
_____

S M T W T F S

PRAYER REQUESTS

- _____
- _____
- _____
- _____
- _____
- _____

SCRIPTURE REFERENCES

_____
_____
_____
_____
_____
_____

GOD'S RESPONSE

_____
_____
_____
_____
_____
_____

If ye shall ask any thing in my name, I will do it.

JOHN 14:14

Stones of Remembrance

DATE _____

S M T W T F S

ANSWERED PRAYER

REMEMBRANCE

_____
_____
_____
_____

ANSWERED PRAYER

REMEMBRANCE

_____
_____
_____
_____

> Then shall ye call upon me, and ye shall go and pray unto me, and I will hearken unto you.
> **JEREMIAH 29:12**

PRAYER JOURNAL
Day 63

DATE _____

S M T W T F S

PRAYER REQUESTS

- _____
- _____
- _____
- _____
- _____
- _____

SCRIPTURE REFERENCES

_____
_____
_____
_____
_____
_____

GOD'S RESPONSE

_____
_____
_____
_____
_____
_____
_____

 Ask, and it shall be given you; seek, and ye shall find; knock, and it shall be opened unto you
MATTHEW 7:7

DATE

S M T W T F S

ANSWERED PRAYER

REMEMBRANCE

ANSWERED PRAYER

REMEMBRANCE

> "For every one that asketh receiveth; and he that seeketh findeth; and to him that knocketh it shall be opened.
> MATTHEW 7:8"

PRAYER JOURNAL
Day 64

DATE

S M T W T F S

PRAYER REQUESTS

-
-
-
-
-

SCRIPTURE REFERENCES

GOD'S RESPONSE

 Therefore I say unto you, What things soever ye desire, when ye pray, believe that ye receive them, and ye shall have them.
MARK 11:24 KJV

DATE
S M T W T F S

ANSWERED PRAYER

REMEMBRANCE

ANSWERED PRAYER

REMEMBRANCE

 And if we know that he hear us, whatsoever we ask, we know that we have the petitions that we desired of him.
1 JOHN 5:15

PRAYER JOURNAL
Day 65

DATE

S M T W T F S

PRAYER REQUESTS

-
-
-
-
-
-

SCRIPTURE REFERENCES

_____
_____
_____
_____
_____
_____

GOD'S RESPONSE

_____
_____
_____
_____
_____

> Be careful for nothing; but in every thing by prayer and supplication with thanksgiving let your requests be made known unto God. And the peace of God, which passeth all understanding, shall keep your hearts and minds through Christ Jesus.
>
> **PHILIPPIANS 4:6-7**

DATE

S M T W T F S

ANSWERED PRAYER

REMEMBRANCE

___

ANSWERED PRAYER

REMEMBRANCE

> " But verily God hath heard me; he hath attended to the voice of my prayer. Blessed be God, which hath not turned away my prayer, nor his mercy from me.
>
> PSALM 66:19-20 "

PRAYER JOURNAL
Day 66

DATE _____

S M T W T F S

PRAYER REQUESTS

- _____
- _____
- _____
- _____
- _____

SCRIPTURE REFERENCES

_____
_____
_____
_____
_____
_____

GOD'S RESPONSE

_____
_____
_____
_____
_____
_____

> Call unto me, and I will answer thee, and show thee great and mighty things, which thou knowest not.
>
> JEREMIAH 33:3

DATE

S M T W T F S

ANSWERED PRAYER

REMEMBRANCE

ANSWERED PRAYER

REMEMBRANCE

 For the eyes of the Lord are over the righteous, and his ears are open unto their prayers: but the face of the Lord is against them that do evil.
1 PETER 3:12

PRAYER JOURNAL
Day 67

DATE _____

S M T W T F S

PRAYER REQUESTS

- _____
- _____
- _____
- _____
- _____
- _____

SCRIPTURE REFERENCES

_____
_____
_____
_____
_____
_____

GOD'S RESPONSE

_____
_____
_____
_____
_____
_____

> "And all things, whatsoever ye shall ask in prayer, believing, ye shall receive.
> MATTHEW 21:22"

DATE
_____
S M T W T F S

ANSWERED PRAYER

REMEMBRANCE

_____
_____
_____
_____

ANSWERED PRAYER

REMEMBRANCE

_____
_____
_____
_____

 The righteous cry, and the LORD heareth, and delivereth them out of all their troubles.
PSALM 34:17

PRAYER JOURNAL
Day 68

DATE _____

S M T W T F S

PRAYER REQUESTS

- _____
- _____
- _____
- _____
- _____
- _____

SCRIPTURE REFERENCES

_____
_____
_____
_____
_____
_____

GOD'S RESPONSE

_____
_____
_____
_____
_____
_____

> And whatsoever we ask, we receive of him, because we keep his commandments, and do those things that are pleasing in his sight.
> 1 JOHN 3:22

DATE _____

S M T W T F S

ANSWERED PRAYER

REMEMBRANCE

_____
_____
_____
_____

ANSWERED PRAYER

REMEMBRANCE

_____
_____
_____
_____

> " O thou that hearest prayer, unto thee shall all flesh come.
> PSALM 65:2 "

PRAYER JOURNAL
Day 69

DATE _____

S M T W T F S

PRAYER REQUESTS

- _____
- _____
- _____
- _____
- _____
- _____

SCRIPTURE REFERENCES

GOD'S RESPONSE

> If ye shall ask any thing in my name, I will do it.
> JOHN 14:14

DATE
S M T W T F S

ANSWERED PRAYER

REMEMBRANCE

ANSWERED PRAYER

REMEMBRANCE

 Then shall ye call upon me, and ye shall go and pray unto me, and I will hearken unto you.
JEREMIAH 29:12

PRAYER JOURNAL
Day 70

DATE

S M T W T F S

PRAYER REQUESTS

-
-
-
-
-
-

SCRIPTURE REFERENCES

___
___
___
___
___
___

GOD'S RESPONSE

___
___
___
___
___
___

Ask, and it shall be given you; seek, and ye shall find; knock, and it shall be opened unto you
MATTHEW 7:7

DATE _____

S M T W T F S

ANSWERED PRAYER

REMEMBRANCE

ANSWERED PRAYER

REMEMBRANCE

> "For every one that asketh receiveth; and he that seeketh findeth; and to him that knocketh it shall be opened.
> MATTHEW 7:8"

PRAYER JOURNAL
Day 71

DATE _____

S M T W T F S

PRAYER REQUESTS

- _____
- _____
- _____
- _____
- _____
- _____

SCRIPTURE REFERENCES

_____
_____
_____
_____
_____
_____

GOD'S RESPONSE

_____
_____
_____
_____
_____
_____

> Therefore I say unto you, What things soever ye desire, when ye pray, believe that ye receive them, and ye shall have them.
>
> MARK 11:24 KJV

Stones of Remembrance

DATE _____

S M T W T F S

ANSWERED PRAYER

REMEMBRANCE

ANSWERED PRAYER

REMEMBRANCE

 And if we know that he hear us, whatsoever we ask, we know that we have the petitions that we desired of him.
1 JOHN 5:15

PRAYER JOURNAL
Day 72

DATE _____

S M T W T F S

PRAYER REQUESTS

- _____
- _____
- _____
- _____
- _____
- _____

SCRIPTURE REFERENCES

_____
_____
_____
_____
_____
_____

GOD'S RESPONSE

_____
_____
_____
_____
_____

> "Be careful for nothing; but in every thing by prayer and supplication with thanksgiving let your requests be made known unto God. And the peace of God, which passeth all understanding, shall keep your hearts and minds through Christ Jesus."
>
> **PHILIPPIANS 4:6-7**

DATE _____

S M T W T F S

ANSWERED PRAYER

REMEMBRANCE

_____
_____
_____

ANSWERED PRAYER

REMEMBRANCE

_____
_____
_____

> "But verily God hath heard me; he hath attended to the voice of my prayer. Blessed be God, which hath not turned away my prayer, nor his mercy from me.
>
> PSALM 66:19-20"

PRAYER JOURNAL
Day 73

DATE _____

S M T W T F S

PRAYER REQUESTS

- _____
- _____
- _____
- _____
- _____
- _____

SCRIPTURE REFERENCES

_____
_____
_____
_____
_____
_____

GOD'S RESPONSE

_____
_____
_____
_____
_____

 Call unto me, and I will answer thee, and show thee great and mighty things, which thou knowest not.
JEREMIAH 33:3

DATE _____

S M T W T F S

ANSWERED PRAYER

REMEMBRANCE

ANSWERED PRAYER

REMEMBRANCE

 For the eyes of the Lord are over the righteous, and his ears are open unto their prayers: but the face of the Lord is against them that do evil.
1 PETER 3:12

PRAYER JOURNAL
Day 74

DATE _____

S M T W T F S

PRAYER REQUESTS

- _____
- _____
- _____
- _____
- _____

SCRIPTURE REFERENCES

_____
_____
_____
_____
_____
_____

GOD'S RESPONSE

_____
_____
_____
_____
_____
_____

> And all things, whatsoever ye shall ask in prayer, believing, ye shall receive.
> MATTHEW 21:22

DATE _____

S M T W T F S

ANSWERED PRAYER

REMEMBRANCE

ANSWERED PRAYER

REMEMBRANCE

 The righteous cry, and the LORD heareth, and delivereth them out of all their troubles.
PSALM 34:17

PRAYER JOURNAL
Day 75

DATE

S M T W T F S

PRAYER REQUESTS

- _____
- _____
- _____
- _____
- _____
- _____

SCRIPTURE REFERENCES

_____
_____
_____
_____
_____
_____

GOD'S RESPONSE

_____
_____
_____
_____
_____
_____

> And whatsoever we ask, we receive of him, because we keep his commandments, and do those things that are pleasing in his sight.
> 1 JOHN 3:22

DATE

S M T W T F S

ANSWERED PRAYER

REMEMBRANCE

___
___
___
___

ANSWERED PRAYER

REMEMBRANCE

___
___
___
___

 O thou that hearest prayer, unto thee shall all flesh come.
PSALM 65:2

PRAYER JOURNAL
Day 76

DATE _____

S M T W T F S

PRAYER REQUESTS

- _____
- _____
- _____
- _____
- _____
- _____

SCRIPTURE REFERENCES

_____
_____
_____
_____
_____
_____

GOD'S RESPONSE

_____
_____
_____
_____
_____
_____

 If ye shall ask any thing in my name, I will do it.
JOHN 14:14

Stones of Remembrance

DATE _____

S   M   T   W   T   F   S

ANSWERED PRAYER

REMEMBRANCE

_____
_____
_____
_____

ANSWERED PRAYER

REMEMBRANCE

_____
_____
_____
_____

Then shall ye call upon me, and ye shall go and pray unto me, and I will hearken unto you.

JEREMIAH 29:12

PRAYER JOURNAL
Day 77

DATE

S M T W T F S

PRAYER REQUESTS

-
-
-
-
-
-

SCRIPTURE REFERENCES

_____
_____
_____
_____
_____
_____

GOD'S RESPONSE

_____
_____
_____
_____
_____
_____

> "Ask, and it shall be given you; seek, and ye shall find; knock, and it shall be opened unto you"
> MATTHEW 7:7

DATE

S M T W T F S

ANSWERED PRAYER

REMEMBRANCE

ANSWERED PRAYER

REMEMBRANCE

> "For every one that asketh receiveth; and he that seeketh findeth; and to him that knocketh it shall be opened.
> MATTHEW 7:8

PRAYER JOURNAL
Day 78

DATE _____

S M T W T F S

PRAYER REQUESTS

- _____
- _____
- _____
- _____
- _____
- _____

SCRIPTURE REFERENCES

_____
_____
_____
_____
_____
_____

GOD'S RESPONSE

_____
_____
_____
_____
_____
_____

Therefore I say unto you, What things soever ye desire, when ye pray, believe that ye receive them, and ye shall have them.
MARK 11:24 KJV

Stones of Remembrance

DATE _____

S M T W T F S

ANSWERED PRAYER

REMEMBRANCE

_____
_____
_____
_____

ANSWERED PRAYER

REMEMBRANCE

_____
_____
_____
_____

 And if we know that he hear us, whatsoever we ask, we know that we have the petitions that we desired of him.
1 JOHN 5:15

PRAYER JOURNAL
Day 79

DATE

S M T W T F S

PRAYER REQUESTS

-
-
-
-
-
-

SCRIPTURE REFERENCES

_____
_____
_____
_____
_____
_____

GOD'S RESPONSE

_____
_____
_____
_____
_____

> " Be careful for nothing; but in every thing by prayer and supplication with thanksgiving let your requests be made known unto God. And the peace of God, which passeth all understanding, shall keep your hearts and minds through Christ Jesus.
>
> **PHILIPPIANS 4:6-7**

DATE

S M T W T F S

ANSWERED PRAYER

REMEMBRANCE

ANSWERED PRAYER

REMEMBRANCE

> "But verily God hath heard me; he hath attended to the voice of my prayer. Blessed be God, which hath not turned away my prayer, nor his mercy from me."
>
> PSALM 66:19-20

PRAYER JOURNAL
Day 80

DATE

S M T W T F S

PRAYER REQUESTS

- _____
- _____
- _____

- _____
- _____
- _____

SCRIPTURE REFERENCES

_____
_____
_____
_____
_____
_____
_____

GOD'S RESPONSE

_____
_____
_____
_____
_____
_____
_____

 Call unto me, and I will answer thee, and show thee great and mighty things, which thou knowest not.
JEREMIAH 33:3

Stones of Remembrance

DATE _____

S M T W T F S

ANSWERED PRAYER

REMEMBRANCE

_____
_____
_____
_____

ANSWERED PRAYER

REMEMBRANCE

_____
_____
_____
_____

> "For the eyes of the Lord are over the righteous, and his ears are open unto their prayers: but the face of the Lord is against them that do evil.
> 1 PETER 3:12"

PRAYER JOURNAL
Day 81

DATE _____

S M T W T F S

PRAYER REQUESTS

- _____
- _____
- _____
- _____
- _____
- _____

SCRIPTURE REFERENCES

_____
_____
_____
_____
_____
_____

GOD'S RESPONSE

_____
_____
_____
_____
_____
_____
_____

And all things, whatsoever ye shall ask in prayer, believing, ye shall receive.
MATTHEW 21:22

DATE _____

S M T W T F S

ANSWERED PRAYER

REMEMBRANCE

_____
_____
_____
_____

ANSWERED PRAYER

REMEMBRANCE

_____
_____
_____
_____

> "The righteous cry, and the LORD heareth, and delivereth them out of all their troubles."
> **PSALM 34:17**

PRAYER JOURNAL
Day 82

DATE _____

S M T W T F S

PRAYER REQUESTS

- _____
- _____
- _____

- _____
- _____
- _____

SCRIPTURE REFERENCES

_____
_____
_____
_____
_____
_____

GOD'S RESPONSE

_____
_____
_____
_____
_____
_____

> And whatsoever we ask, we receive of him, because we keep his commandments, and do those things that are pleasing in his sight.
> 1 JOHN 3:22

DATE _____

S M T W T F S

ANSWERED PRAYER

REMEMBRANCE

ANSWERED PRAYER

REMEMBRANCE

 O thou that hearest prayer, unto thee shall all flesh come.
PSALM 65:2

PRAYER JOURNAL
Day 83

DATE

S M T W T F S

PRAYER REQUESTS

- _____
- _____
- _____
- _____
- _____
- _____

SCRIPTURE REFERENCES

_____
_____
_____
_____
_____
_____

GOD'S RESPONSE

_____
_____
_____
_____
_____
_____

> If ye shall ask any thing in my name, I will do it.
> JOHN 14:14

Stones of Remembrance

DATE _____

S M T W T F S

ANSWERED PRAYER

REMEMBRANCE

_____
_____
_____
_____

ANSWERED PRAYER

REMEMBRANCE

_____
_____
_____
_____

> Then shall ye call upon me, and ye shall go and pray unto me, and I will hearken unto you.
> **JEREMIAH 29:12**

PRAYER JOURNAL
Day 84

DATE
_____

S M T W T F S

PRAYER REQUESTS

- _____
- _____
- _____
- _____
- _____
- _____

SCRIPTURE REFERENCES

_____
_____
_____
_____
_____
_____

GOD'S RESPONSE

_____
_____
_____
_____
_____
_____

Ask, and it shall be given you; seek, and ye shall find; knock, and it shall be opened unto you

MATTHEW 7:7

DATE _____

S M T W T F S

ANSWERED PRAYER

REMEMBRANCE

_____
_____
_____
_____

ANSWERED PRAYER

REMEMBRANCE

_____
_____
_____
_____

> "For every one that asketh receiveth; and he that seeketh findeth; and to him that knocketh it shall be opened.
> MATTHEW 7:8"

PRAYER JOURNAL
Day 85

DATE _____

S M T W T F S

PRAYER REQUESTS

- _____
- _____
- _____
- _____
- _____
- _____

SCRIPTURE REFERENCES

_____
_____
_____
_____
_____
_____

GOD'S RESPONSE

_____
_____
_____
_____
_____
_____

> Therefore I say unto you, What things soever ye desire, when ye pray, believe that ye receive them, and ye shall have them.
>
> MARK 11:24 KJV

DATE _____

S M T W T F S

ANSWERED PRAYER

REMEMBRANCE

_____
_____
_____
_____

ANSWERED PRAYER

REMEMBRANCE

_____
_____
_____
_____

 And if we know that he hear us, whatsoever we ask, we know that we have the petitions that we desired of him.
1 JOHN 5:15

PRAYER JOURNAL
Day 86

DATE

S M T W T F S

PRAYER REQUESTS

-
-
-
-
-
-

SCRIPTURE REFERENCES

_____
_____
_____
_____
_____
_____

GOD'S RESPONSE

_____
_____
_____
_____
_____

> "Be careful for nothing; but in every thing by prayer and supplication with thanksgiving let your requests be made known unto God. And the peace of God, which passeth all understanding, shall keep your hearts and minds through Christ Jesus.
>
> PHILIPPIANS 4:6-7

DATE _____

S M T W T F S

ANSWERED PRAYER

REMEMBRANCE

_____
_____
_____

ANSWERED PRAYER

REMEMBRANCE

_____
_____
_____

> "But verily God hath heard me; he hath attended to the voice of my prayer. Blessed be God, which hath not turned away my prayer, nor his mercy from me.
>
> PSALM 66:19-20"

PRAYER JOURNAL
Day 87

DATE _____

S M T W T F S

PRAYER REQUESTS

- _____
- _____
- _____
- _____
- _____

SCRIPTURE REFERENCES

_____
_____
_____
_____
_____
_____

GOD'S RESPONSE

_____
_____
_____
_____
_____
_____

> *Call unto me, and I will answer thee, and show thee great and mighty things, which thou knowest not.*
> **JEREMIAH 33:3**

DATE

S M T W T F S

ANSWERED PRAYER

REMEMBRANCE

_____
_____
_____
_____

ANSWERED PRAYER

REMEMBRANCE

_____
_____
_____
_____

> "For the eyes of the Lord are over the righteous, and his ears are open unto their prayers: but the face of the Lord is against them that do evil.
> 1 PETER 3:12

PRAYER JOURNAL
Day 88

DATE

S M T W T F S

PRAYER REQUESTS

-
-
-
-
-
-

SCRIPTURE REFERENCES

GOD'S RESPONSE

And all things, whatsoever ye shall ask in prayer, believing, ye shall receive.
MATTHEW 21:22

DATE

S M T W T F S

ANSWERED PRAYER

REMBERANCE

ANSWERED PRAYER

REMEMBRANCE

> " The righteous cry, and the LORD heareth, and delivereth them out of all their troubles.
> PSALM 34:17 "

PRAYER JOURNAL
Day 89

DATE

S M T W T F S

PRAYER REQUESTS

- _____
- _____
- _____
- _____
- _____
- _____

SCRIPTURE REFERENCES

_____
_____
_____
_____
_____
_____

GOD'S RESPONSE

_____
_____
_____
_____
_____
_____

> And whatsoever we ask, we receive of him, because we keep his commandments, and do those things that are pleasing in his sight.
> 1 JOHN 3:22

DATE
S M T W T F S

ANSWERED PRAYER

REMEMBRANCE

ANSWERED PRAYER

REMEMBRANCE

 O thou that hearest prayer, unto thee shall all flesh come.
PSALM 65:2

PRAYER JOURNAL
Day 90

DATE _____

S M T W T F S

PRAYER REQUESTS

- _____
- _____
- _____

- _____
- _____
- _____

SCRIPTURE REFERENCES

_____
_____
_____
_____
_____
_____

GOD'S RESPONSE

_____
_____
_____
_____
_____
_____

If ye shall ask any thing in my name, I will do it.

JOHN 14:14

DATE

S M T W T F S

ANSWERED PRAYER

REMEMBRANCE

ANSWERED PRAYER

REMEMBRANCE

Then shall ye call upon me, and ye shall go and pray unto me, and I will hearken unto you.
JEREMIAH 29:12

Congratulations!

You've completed 90 days of prayer! Now, begin again.

But without faith it is impossible to please Him, for whoever comes [near] to God must [necessarily] believe that God exists and that He rewards those who [earnestly and diligently] seek Him.

HEBREWS 11:6 AMP

The Stones of Remembrance Journal is lovingly dedicated to my Aunt, Pastor Janice K. Chimney.

Throughout the years, Aunt Janice has stood as a powerful intercessor, faithfully lifting the needs of others in prayer. I honor her commitment to prayer, and I am thankful that years ago, she introduced me to the idea of chronicling answered prayers.

With deep appreciation and gratitude, I dedicate this journal to Aunt Janice, acknowledging the impact she's had on the lives of many.

Made in the USA
Las Vegas, NV
08 July 2023

74392281R00105